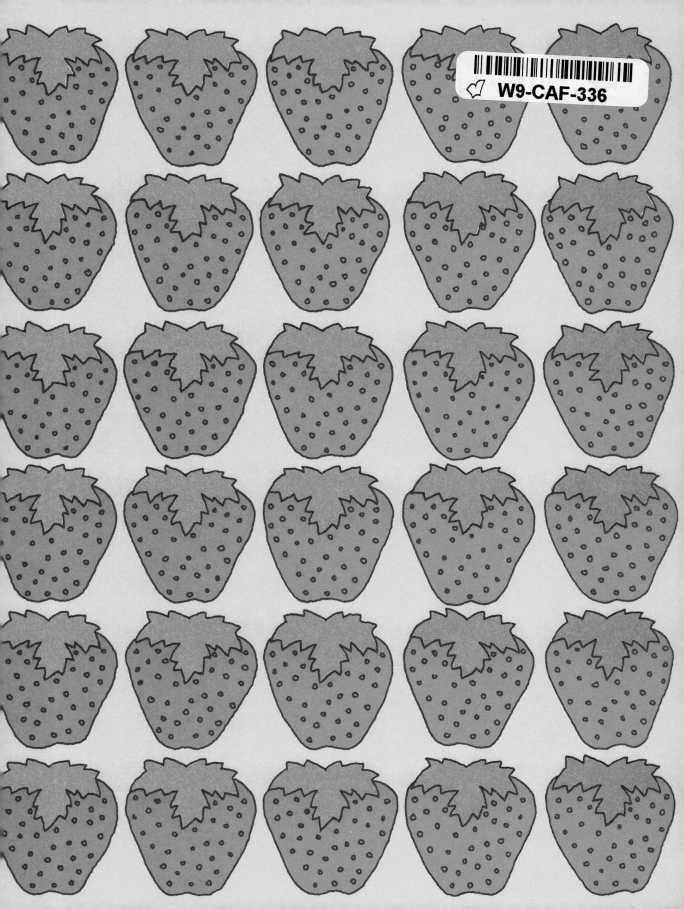

THE STICKYBEAR FAMILY ™

Bedford Stickybear   **Sara Stickybear**
Bumper Stickybear

this
strawberry library
of first learning
book
belongs to

Stickybear™ is the registered trademark of Optimum Resource, Inc.
Strawberry® and A Strawberry Book® are the registered
trademarks of One Strawberry, Inc.

Weekly Reader Books' Edition

Library of Congress Cataloging in Publication Data

Hefter, Richard.
    Jobs for bears.

    (Stickybear books)
    ''Weekly Reader Books' edition.''
    Summary: Shows bears engaged in a variety of oc-
cupations.
    1. Occupations – Juvenile literature.   [1. Occupa-
tions] I. Title.   II. Series: Hefter, Richard.
Stickybear books.
HF5382.H43   1983   331.7'02   83-2197
ISBN 0-911787-02-X

jobs
for bears

by Richard Hefter

Optimum Resource, Inc. • Connecticut

We're going to show you all the different jobs we do!

cart collector

FAST CHECK

bagger

checkout cashier

store manager

CLOSED

We work in a supermarket.

We love to work with computers.

maintenance person

terminal operator

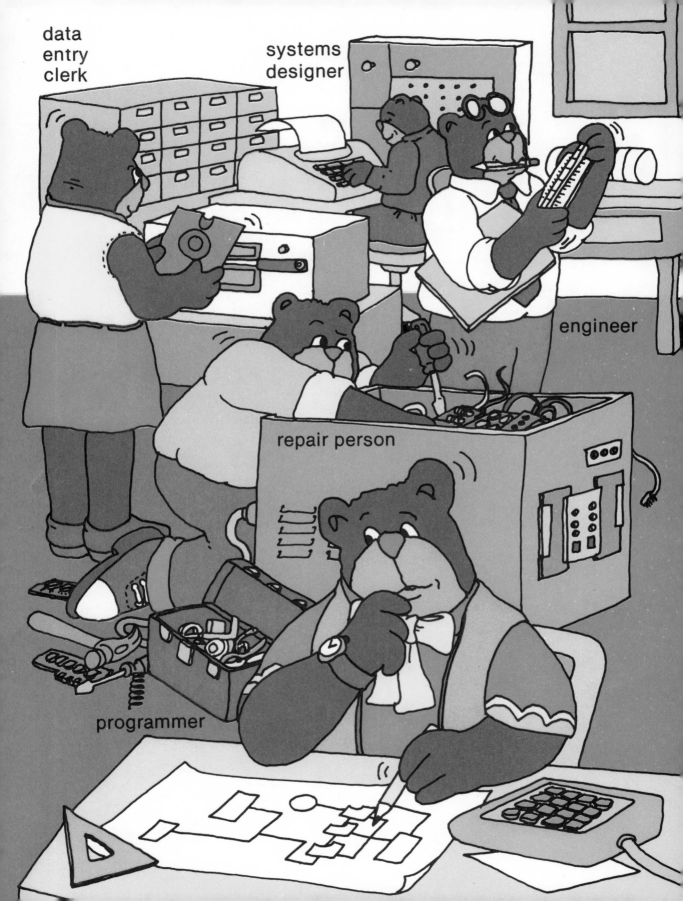

Our job is taking care of everyone.

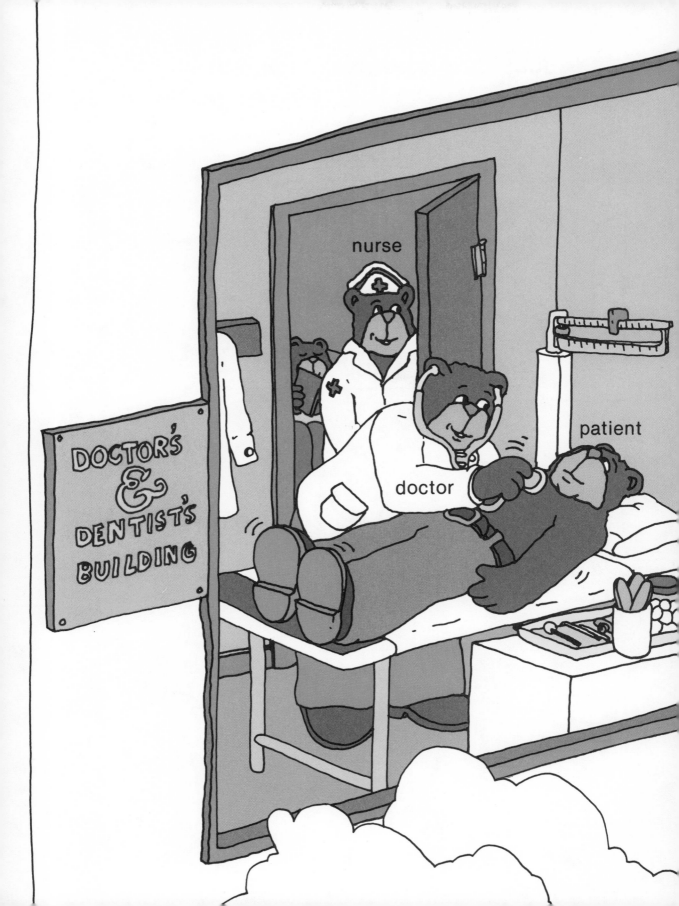

Feeding hungry people is our job!

fire fighters

FIRE DEPARTMENT

fire fighter

fire fighter

fire fighter

fire fighters

fire chief

fire fighter

firehouse dog

workers

supervisor

plant
manager

worker

quality
inspector

workers

robot

forewoman

worker

SPRAY BOOTH

We work in a factory.

planter

farmer

pickers

We work on a farm.

loader

feeder

milker

We work in an amusement park.

animal trainer

trained dog

HOT DOGS

hot dog salesperson

ride operator

SODA

CANDY

COME ON IN

clown

balloon seller

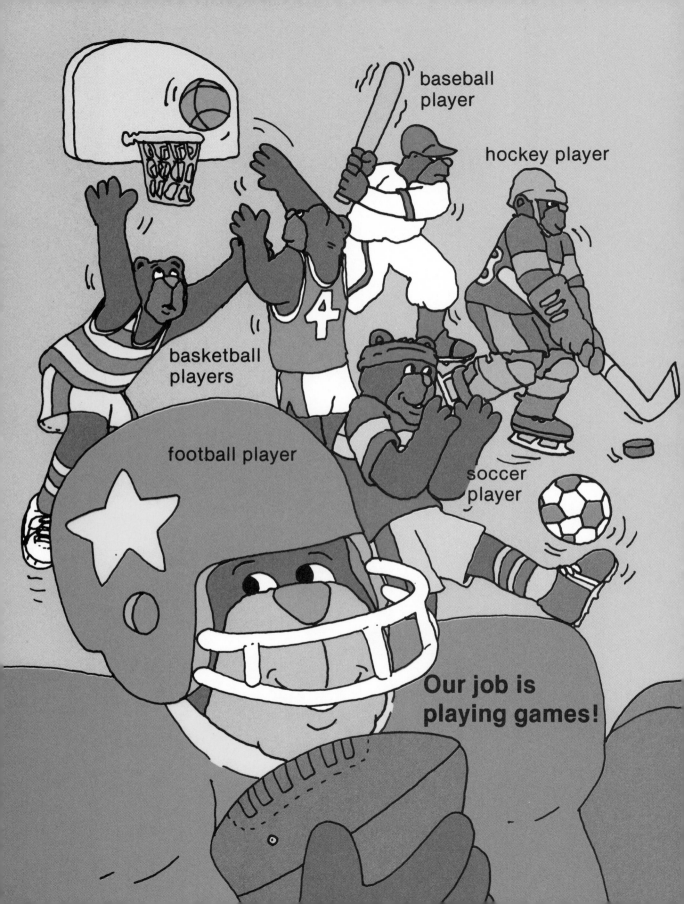

emergency crew

food service crew

BEAR AIR

We work at the airport.

air traffic
controller

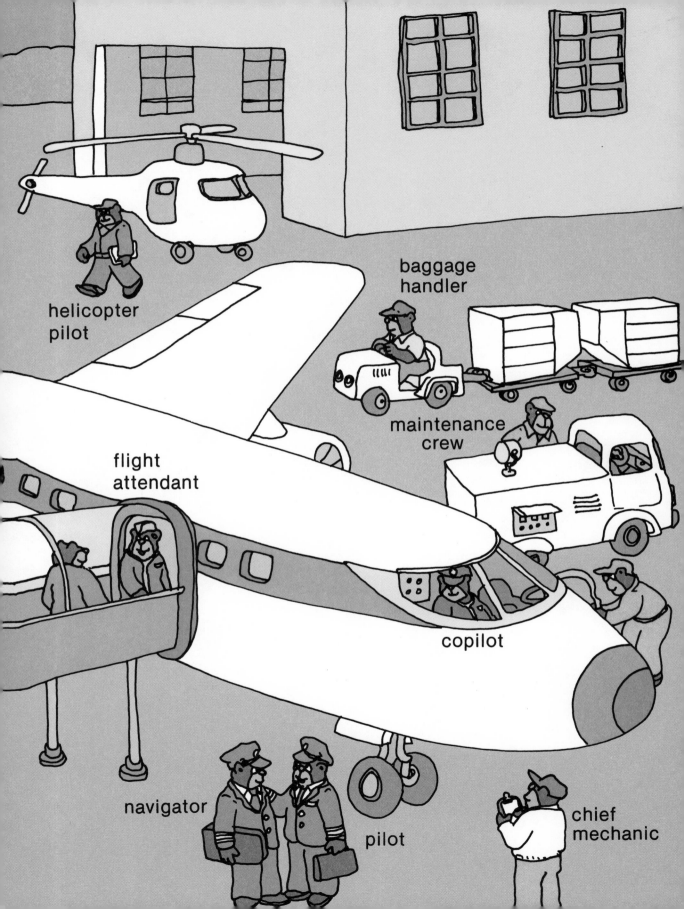

helicopter
pilot

baggage
handler

maintenance
crew

flight
attendant

copilot

navigator

pilot

chief
mechanic